LIVING QUARTERS

ALSO BY ADRIENNE SU

MIDDLE KINGDOM
SANCTUARY
HAVING NONE OF IT

LIVING QUARTERS

ADRIENNE SU

MANIC D PRESS
SAN FRANCISCO

FOR
PEOPLE AND ANIMALS
WHO HAVE NO HOME

Living Quarters ©2015 by Adrienne Su. All rights reserved. Published by
Manic D Press. For information, contact Manic D Press, PO Box 410804,
San Francisco CA 94141 www.manicdpress.com   Printed in Canada

Library of Congress Cataloging-in-Publication Data

Su, Adrienne, 1967-
  [Poems. Selections]
  Living quarters / Adrienne Su.
pages ; cm
ISBN 978-1-933149-89-9 (trade pbk. original : alk. paper)
I. Title.
PS3569.U13A6 2015
811'.54--dc23

                              2014044711

CONTENTS

I

II

III

IV

I

The door itself
makes no promises.
It is only a door.

– Adrienne Rich

Earthbound

If anticipation
is the high point of travel,
we ought to vacation
at home, reading manuals,

marking vintage hotels
and undiscovered vistas,
composing the meals
strangers will make us,

just as, lacking money,
I once took Italian
at the state university,
cooked from Marcella Hazan,

dipped in and out of Dante.
Although it was Iowa City,
that summer still resonates
as the summer of Italy.

I distinguished myself in class
by having no plans to travel.
Others were making it happen,
flying standby, lodging in hostels.

I must have wanted a kingdom
I could build in office or kitchen,
then be home by bedtime,
closing my eyes for vision.

Chinese Parsley

I never call it that.
It evokes too freely: checkers,
fire drill, ancient secret,
zodiac, laundry, whispers.

Does my culinary self
object, because it isn't
parsley, or my research self,
because its homeland isn't

China? One could venture
it has spent enough centuries
there to be considered
citizen. It goes so speedily

to seed, that's thousands
of generations. If pressed
to explain my aversion
to the term, I would attest

to the difficulty, amid
shoppers and vegetables,
of trying to decide – *is this
a taco / biryani / spring-roll*

*week, or is it minestrone /
steak / roast chicken?* – when
all shorthand ends in parsley.
Cilantro's the better partition.

Contentment

On obvious levels I long for it: daily
domestic certainty, light, familiarity,
the family dog, family. I see an armchair
reserved for the man (though that's not fair),
a kitchen where pots are always astir,
clamoring little ones, invasions at Easter
and Christmas by in-laws, out-of-tune crowds
on birthdays, board games, sporting goods,
and downstairs or up, room for a child
who's glimpsed her purpose to hide,
unseen but not unhappy, for most of the party.
As mother, I don't see myself at all, in part
because the self is invisible outside mirrors
and photographs, in part because I'll never
occupy that house, having found the sacred
space in my day, known what it had sentenced
me to, and accepted with the unequivocal
ease of a girl just old enough and viable.

1980

Mostly we waited, playing cards or *Sorry!*
in the basement, while the parents sipped tea
above us, salted melon seeds, dried plums,
and husks mounding up in the table's center.
They spoke both languages; we spoke one;
we intended them to live forever.

That summer we had biked up and down
the neighborhood hills, earned permission
to cross one highway, and come around
to the normal contradictions, matters
of age and location. We could say it now:
what we shared was not as it appeared.

Dinner over, night coming on, we switched
to Monopoly. It lasted too long; the frigid
damp moved into our skinny frames.
We went upstairs, nibbled the occasional
plum, left the pit. The grownups sent us away,
switched dialects, laughed at untranslatable

anecdotes. That was the era when
we felt like tagalongs, too old to run
along and play, too young to go alone.
Later, dragged to Oriental Provision,
which smelled of fish and scallions,
we tiptoed around the owners' children,

who wandered the aisles with dirty feet,
downcast faces, and nothing to read.
We didn't all associate at school but usually
said hello. Only the parents were positioned
to fall into the circle – mirthful, otherworldly –
and seem to travel. We never made it in.

Kitchen

Site of dumpling party,
camp of holiday labor,

invaded by loose-leaf,
snack site, bar, pet station,

it makes dinner possible
but never makes dinner.

Kingdom of creative potential,
it has drained creative potential

for centuries. Now stocked
with life-source that, neglected,

turns sickness-source,
it has no proprietor,

only guest chefs who double
as guests. Yet its rituals

still reanimate all
who come from other rooms,

even if they're grandmothers
or look like grandmothers

or know their way around.
Microwave, dishwasher, kettle:

they may do only one thing well
(or two), but let us let them try.

A room shall never own a person.
It is only a room.

Sunday Dinner

As if I didn't have real work to do.
As if I had envisioned the nation my parents had.
As if the elders hadn't promised something new.

I was confident, like other women, like children.
It couldn't swallow me; I had had a chance to refuse.
And what I wanted was innocuous and common:

Everyone at a single table – never mind the unfinished
papers, taking up a place. The gravy boat we never used.
Now, as we flailed in the sea, it would have to float us.

Salvation didn't happen, by ritual or rite.
The tragedy gathered slowly, litter on the road.
Babies wailed. Hungry all the time, lacking appetite,

I was finally ready. Someone said it in my head.
I'd do it myself. Red meat. Saturday. Whoever was left.
Just me? I was damned if I couldn't consume that much flesh.

Asian Shrimp

What brute reduced forty-seven countries
and the foods of four billion to an entrée
so named? I prefer not to know, for the answer
will be too close: someone I already treasure
or passingly greet, who's dwelled from birth
in my adopted town, who as a youth unearthed
a glittering kingdom interred in a remaindered
cookbook, then dreamed of it nightly but never
went, yet worked to bring a shadow of a replica
of what it seemed to be, to Dutch Pennsylvania.

At the Checkout

they almost always pause to ask the names
of greens: bok choy, collards, mizuna, mâche.
Today I'm rung up by sweet-faced teenage
JAMES, who scans at speed until he's stopped

by the broccoli rabe. "What's this?" he mutters,
and I nearly choke on the ways it is exalted –
with pancetta on penne, with clams, smothered
in garlic, souffléed, or blanched and salted –

while he enters the code. "Oh, baby broccoli,"
he reads, and rolls it out of his life. It's not my age
or how I see, but how I fail and fail again to be,
that blinds me to what James perceives: *broccoli babe.*

Supermarket Fruits

Instead of ripening, they rot,
covertly, from the center.
Kiwi, mango, peach, pear
imitate what they are not,
fragrant lures for animals.
Obdurate, the fruits take on
the manner of a faux Cézanne,
ubiquitous, pretty, inedible.
Bought for their persuasive skins,
they betray the trusting tongue:
bitter, tannic, tart, long gone.
If only we were false like them,
we could use our perfect faces
to infiltrate private spaces.

When More Is Better

First all the critters must have your attention.
The animals are easier, not requiring reasons,
but the children have complexity. The interval
before they wake is always parenthetical,
unusable for news or meditation. Lunch
must be made, shoes found. You're old enough
to know the alternative: days of silence, yielding
more silence, plus anxiety. Sometimes feeling
lost, you ask your self rhetorically what
she might do if you were found. She'd speak, but
she's asleep. You were warned about all of it,
but all of it was in you, looking for an exit.
When no one demanded your life, you gave it over
anyway, to whoever was nearby. All was better
when you made someone, and someone else,
tiny, hungry. Sometimes when sleep is scarce
and you've exploded your dowdiness quotient,
you dream of paradise, but where? At the Giant,
pushing the cart of offspring and perishables,
mentally packing your rucksack of breakables
and dry-clean-onlys, you know how the story
would end. It wouldn't even be literary.

Dessert

One day we'll be inconsolable by sugar.
Non-nourishing? Non-essential? Whoever
says it surely lines up ducks so as to strike
them down with neither grief nor appetite.

In Late November

Having spurned the anonymous frozen hulks
in supermarket rows, we're face to face
or face to beak with knowledge: we plan to salt
a bird that, down the street, still starts each day

without foreboding, as if being moved from grass
to grass to eat, then eat, were a human benevolence,
a gift from strong to meek. The kindest path.
Yet when the day arrives, despite not having met

the flock, I wake in dread, aware of my nature.
I've been staying up late, planning the feast,
what to do with the leftover flesh, as the Mayflower
tale unfolds for the next generation. At least

now they include some gore (just a smidgen:
boat diseased, some deaths). Meeting the farmer,
I picture the hundred dismembered chickens
I've known only as limbs this year and wonder

which of my crimes is the worst. "You can't
get a fresher bird," he says. "This turkey
was walking around this morning." A pang
illuminates the absent-minded grocery

runs I make all year. For what are we thankful?
A roof, hot meals, each other, the possible end
of two wars. Gratitude mixes with animal
feelings or thoughts, whatever they are when

they come without words. It's my favorite
holiday – no gifts, no faith or its baggage –
but it too has its tidy scriptures, an edited
version for children. I take the package.

The Wife

She was nothing. I was she. Even
though she understood, the pouring
of silvery light into the kitchen
each brisk newlywed morning,

the crackling of loaves being lifted
from the stone, the blackness of tea
made days unfold as if divinely scripted,
as if all were a discipline, universally

obeyed. The lack of plans, the hunger
of the ocean, the slight uncertainty
about necessities created neither
fear nor worry; all who were officially

we would find their way. A man
would protect his home. The community
had ratified it; there were documents.
In many directions lay the imagery

of peace: the neighbors' quince trees,
orderly gardens, dogs who never
gave chase. There was ambiguity
of duty, money was tight, failures

went unassigned, but many had lived
with worse. Each day yielded a little
more peace. The rain let up, or fuzzy mist
shrouded the hills, which were beautiful.

Like the tide, like the sun going pink
and waning while she boned the bird
or turned the carrots, the radio her link
to agents of consequence, it unfurled,

her life, theirs. What was meant
to happen did, and just as in
any accident, they'd later count
the hundred ways it might have been

better, less violent, or more profound.

Rosemary

Its name, compound of two, belies
the spikiness, assertive oil, power
to overtake. If it ever symbolized

rule by woman, I didn't know, even
as I nurtured one in bonsai form
while living like half a citizen;

of course it withered. It also carried
odors of memory, loyalty; brides
wore it in garlands; it was buried

with certain dead. Having treated it
as seasoning, I earned its desertion,
snipping too literally, only to eat it

(white beans, roast potatoes, lamb).
Its mystique dissolved like a woman's:
neglected, turned colleague, custodian,

kitchen standby, bereft of desire,
it first dropped leaves, then paled despite
textbook care. I wrote off the failure

as bonsai fussiness, my ungreen thumb,
even as I moved from town to town,
convinced the magical day would come

when everything was transferred:
from story to myth, renter to owner,
early to late, tentative to empowered.

II

Grown, and miles from home, why do I shy
From every anonymous door-slam or dull eye?

– Jean Valentine

II

Turning in Early

Part centering of gravity,
part renouncing of company,
better in winter
but feasible always,
the aim is living larger
by private destination,
getting ahead of the sun.
So much is broken
by daylight that refuses
to reconcile,
rest may resist,
breath forget its depth,
but the site of forgetting
reassembles parts.
Seeming to end,
everything starts.
To prostrate the body
despite upright ideas
exudes the sureness
observers envy, watching
you ascend alone as if
to an appointment to which
they're never invited,
although you go so early
out of knowledge,
out of mercy.

Leisure

There's no man to see, no dog about which.
Too easy to accuse the innocent, forget

to wake up, attend to aches. I worked for this,
imagined, saved, emptied rooms for what

was clearly sacred; those I asked to get lost
got lost. Now all surfaces are clean,

lists go straight to essentials, the ghost
existence that underlay the quotidian

floats to the top – so what are these lines
on the page, those calls from outside

that grate, their edge demonic, feline?
Something unfinished draws my eye

to the door. If there were a knock,
I'd be making a choice, though common,

to burrow, interior, or stand and talk,
the business self I used to summon

and command. It would be a local candidate,
salesperson, church – no Trojan horse –

but even if I fled in outsize agitation,
the flight would be deliberate, exerting force.

Complaint

Does the pain manifest in neck, hip, shoulders, head?
Would you call it chronic, or do you suffer isolated
spasms of distress, such as a damsel might express upon
tiedness to tracks, till she's stretched, slashed, or undone
the ropes? Does trivia dog you, such as whether the word
"ambivalent" has one stressed syllable or two, as heard
in the solar plexus? Are you depressed or just too able
to apprehend the daily mess: eighty-five people
killed by guns, eighteen hundred women raped,
five thousand dogs put down (this just in the States)?
Confess who you are, attuned to the killer in painkiller,
incapable of rest or pleasure while any suffer.
Knowledge presses on your ears, teeth, stomach, chest,
yet you keep pursuing more, as if it gave you breath.

Insomnia

As if peace and repair were debts
to be repaid promptly, it treats rest

as a privilege, night an offense
to purpose. Even in the absence

of regret, worry at normal levels,
its demons dance. I know the cycle:

best not to marshal the forces
that worked all day, but like horses

they read my mind. Before I decide,
they leave the gate, which is why

I find universities suspect.
At work I'm their advocate

and face, pushing construction
of argument, decontamination

of speech; some call me Doctor
by mistake. Meanwhile I keep after

house dust, hope, a good night's sleep.
Clouds swell; engines rev. Perhaps TV

could burn them out, or a week
out of town, if citizens could leave

the metropolis of thought, cursed,
necessary state. Night could be worse

by so much: that this is gratuitous
makes it extravagantly restless,

the agenda item that always gets me,
resisting the only tool that lets me

pick it up, buzzing as if electric
when its absence is requested.

To Stay in Place

Clean; rearrange; repaint; improve.
It's time, once again, not to move.

Closets shall continue to be few,
so have no mercy, culling shoes.

As the office shall remain an alcove
with imagined door and shelves,

books must be pared to the obscure
and essential. Question all furniture:

when was every chair last sat in?
The kitchen will never be eat-in,

but storage has yet to be maximized:
let hooks and racks assert new life.

Bedrooms still refuse expansion,
but who can sleep in a mansion

whose soaring ceilings would devour
the warm enclosure of the hours

by which all are rejuvenated?
Trading up is overrated:

what you can invent while settled
tests a different kind of mettle.

Bronchitis

It's not a minor illness, but nor is it major:
not much to do but slow down, wait,
and let the present, day by day, turn into future.

Looking forward, not just ahead, to feeling better,
the back of my mind has finally shut the gate.
It's not a minor illness, but nor is it major.

Not to rest is not an option, says the doctor.
Her face adds: *even after this abates.*
Let the present be today and not the future:

extrapolate nothing; sleep; savor pleasure
rather than killing it for being scarce or late.
It's not a minor illness (nor is it major),

but your ailments double if you would sooner
interrogate joy than free it to invade
and turn the present, come what may, into a future.

Will I remember this when I'm recovered
or wipe the trace tranquility away?
It's not a minor illness, but nor is it major.
Today it brought a present, turning off the future.

Affliction

The offense may be small:
an excess of sugar,
lines at the theater,
or traffic, thus late arrival.

No explanation, no appeal.
Someone will pay in regret:
friend, true love, service rep.
Failure burns. It's personal.

We see the same in nations:
enraged by filth of peasants,
foreign accent, animal stench,
tyrants brood in mansions,

finding new forms for power.
But most men lack influence,
subjecting only assistants,
children, intimates, to minor

attacks, with words or silence.
Smart ones never strike.
Cast out, they'd have to fight
affliction alone, its violence

turned inward. When remorse
at last replaces animus,
who will be there, hands
on hips, awaiting the newest

round of talks? The self
being cruelest, the ritual
will hit the stony wall
of breakdown, and what else?

Its rage needs a target
that crumples but always
gets back up, practically
hired for it. Now where was it?

Carlisle, Pennsylvania

Even Gettysburg, which still matters,
isn't that close, so when Hurricane Sandy
set its sights squarely on Cumberland County,
it was notable, briefly, to live in the county.

After the stocking-up and bathtub-filling,
we slept away from windows, which held.
Animals hid from pressure, rain, and wind,
but trees and poles withstood the wind,

which gave the usual inconsequential
beating: clogged gutters, canceled meetings,
a boon for grocers, Home Depot, Target,
the chance to claim we'd been a target –

the modest things we'd bargained for
when we came from coasts and cities
or down the street, and bought our houses,
many a century old, the kind of houses

bathrooms and closets were carved from
later, for our plenitude. A traveler
buying lunch or switching highways
might remark, "There, off the highway,

in that quaint little house, somebody's
whole life is passing," then as quickly
lose the moment's vision of the town
in a swath of country, town, country, town.

Practice

J'ai seize ans, we said all year.
We had longer, more interesting phrases, but that's the one
    that takes me there.
J'ai seize ans, we said all year.
We mulled over college brochures, dismissed the local boys,
    and trained our ears
for distant speech, but there we remained, in geographical
    despair.
We planned to seize the future when it came. We'd know it
    anywhere.
J'ai seize ans, we said all year.

Bathtime

First answer, always: no to getting in.
Then no to getting out. Once we're in,

our mother has to stay, even if she
hurries everything, tries to read,

or sits on the rug with that look
of being gone. But she won't pick

up the phone and has no computer.
Our favorite time. So why fight her?

Baths always seem to come when
something is starting, the moment

we're revving up to stay dry. We're busy.
Bathing isn't life but what constantly

gets in the way, like trying on clothes.
We'd battle harder if we didn't know

the ending: the grownup always wins.
And no matter how much she complains

of exhaustion, she's always happier later
despite still being dirty herself. The water

rises fast, then takes a long time to drain.
It'll be up to us one day, she says again,

when she's old or ruined or dead,
so for now could we please respect

her living wish and wash,
because the world is mostly flesh

(whatever that means: don't try
to picture it) and gone by the time

you're clothed and playing again?
It's mystery enough, we give in.

The Frost Place
Franconia, New Hampshire

The poets drank and declaimed outside
while I stayed in, tied to my body,

recalling, with minimal bitterness,
high school, its odd kisses, missing the party.

At least I had Frost, or the idea of Frost,
to talk to in the dark. And I'd bought

good maternity clothes, culled from racks
so flower-drenched, so vague, I thought

the anxiety, almost rage, of not being me
could harm the baby. But now it was late,

I couldn't be seen, and my mind
clattered and swarmed. What would I make

to eat that week, in Frost's kitchen?
Why hadn't I gone to Europe sooner,

worn hats, kept a place in New York?
Frost's children had eaten one-dish dinners

of boiled potatoes, and not from poverty.
Simplify, I said aloud, or you'll never be

consequential. Laughter from the yard.
I'd heard the joke before, semi-literary.

Out the window, stars caught in screens.
A single road lay ahead, open wide.

All I had to do was shoulder supplies.
All I had to do was provide.

To a Limited Extent

it's not about how far you fall
but how: you could break a leg
by missing what you'd barely call
a height, like the bottom step,

your mind on another planet,
your body dully at home, moving
laundry or a chair. The damage
may be minor, but it quietly ruins

your plans. Never again, you say,
shall I carry laundry or a chair.
For a time you don't, until the day
you have to strive again, to scale

the hill or wall that is the ground,
though still you'd prefer not to lead
this march. (Others have renounced
much more. Everyone needs

to be inert sometimes; could you sit out
further rounds?) Being too strong
enables hope to entwine with doubt
so that both can prove you wrong:

where others would have given in
to joy's unreasonable limits,
you who were always too disciplined
at managing life, managed to miss it.

Into a Rock

After the injury, the teacher instructs:
Come to yoga anyway.
If anything hurts, go into a rock.

Become the ultimate burrower.
Let all be refusal,
not just the center.

The origin of strength
is the will to submit
to requirements of pain,

to curl into limits, imitate
a fossilized animal
immortalized by decay,

dismiss hope of completion,
embrace the body's
response to ambition,

and overthrow the intellect,
which paralyzed
the columns that, cat by cat,

swan by swan, rock by rock,
you seek to reclaim.
Don't even tell it you've stopped.

On Writing

A love poem risks becoming a ruin,
public, irretrievable, a form of tattooing,

while loss, being permanent,
can sustain a thousand documents.

Loss predominates in history,
smorgasbord of death, betrayal, heresy,

crime, contagion, deployment, divorce.
A writer could remain aboard

the ship of grief and thrive, never
approaching the shores of rapture.

What can be said about elation
that the elated, seeking consolation

from their joy, will go to books for?
It's wiser and quicker to look for

a poem in the dentist's chair
than in the luxury suite where

eternal love, declared, turns out
to be eternal. Who cares about

a stranger's bliss? Thus the juncture
where I'm stalled, unaccustomed

to integrity, despite your presence,
our tranquility, and every confidence.

III

his heart is an educated swamp,
and he is mindful of his garden,
which prepares to die.

— Stanley Kunitz

III

Weeding

Uproot them from our nation!
The decisive twist and give
augur transformation:
ragged to tended, anarchic

to formed, almost ruined
to almost beautiful. Wilted piles
molder in bags, destined
for rebirth as matter less reviled,

mulch or dirt to send up fruit.
Less than human, less than plant,
they mustn't reproduce.
Hacked, choked, smothered by hand,

they die for what they represent:
speed, persistence, fecundity.
Anything so successful and abundant
can weather the adversity.

Backyard

I wish I would garden,
wish I had the ambition
to visit my quarter acre
daily, planning nature,

to expand this home
by creating that room,
to cherish not resent
the plot that represents

potential. On the rare
greenhouse visit, I make sure
to inquire: what flowers
can a working single mother

with allergies, back trouble,
and a dog plant in a jungle?
(Sunlight's scarce, too.)
Absurd to ask for blooms,

but my daughters cherish
cut flowers, at which
my immigrant nature rebels:
with land at your disposal,

you undermine the strivings
of generations by buying
what is doomed and can't be eaten.
Is there anything with petals, even

ugly or small, strong enough
to compete in unmulched
beds, those evil plantains
spreading while the humans

read novels or roast a chicken?
I don't expect a true solution.
The answer is not in a nursery.
The answer inhabits the psyche

of the customer who yearns
for nature to have discipline
on someone else's terms,
the consumer who dreams

of unbreakable plates that put
themselves away, pets
that brush their own coats,
children who needn't be told.

That's the would-be gardener
who pays two hundred dollars
for a carful of plants she will kill
all season, day by hot day, until

the lot becomes wild again
and winter returns to even
the fields, shielding every corner
with the same white comforter.

On Being Criticized for Coming from Suburbia

You did not ride your yellow bicycle
a thousand times past the hot-pink azaleas
your father was mulching with pine straw
while your mother set the rice cooker out
in the carport, where it spat hot cooking water,
the lid bobbing in white foam,
initiating evening.

You never walked out the modest French doors
into the brick-walled patio with wrought-iron gates
where you swept leaves in fall, hung clothes in summer.
You didn't dawdle on the backyard swingset
and stare into a sky as infinite as the one above Manhattan
while night came on with fireflies
and the neighbor's dog, always on his side of the fence
and born without a bark, prepared to sleep.

You did not lie down each night knowing
that the journey to this pocket of heaven
with its benevolent dogwoods,
clean sheets, and small chandeliers
had begun decades earlier with the sight of soldiers
marching down every alley,
dragging men to unnamed destinations.
For those not taken, only so long to gather belongings.

No place like a street whose name sounds the same
as the others: Greenbriar, Greenbrook, Greenwillow.
No place like a pristine living room used once a year.
No place like a driveway strewn in spring
with the fallen blossoms of the tulip poplar,
which might as well have been rose petals
as you walked from the mailbox to your castle,
checking for news from the other side.

July

I should have lived like the lettuces and broccoli,
bolting in excessive heat, as nature wills,
instead of pressing onward, making meals,
only to be cut down again, by the one who held me.

Raspberry Patch

Sanguine, swollen,
intending to be taken,
they barely hide, their flesh
the reason for our rash
and burn. Their sweetness
flees as it's apprehended.
Would it be so wrong,
as ankles and wrists succumb
to mosquitoes and nettles,
to long on a primitive level
for the ignorant years
when they simply appeared,
flavorless and beautiful,
whenever we called?
Nothing new in carpe diem
under the terrible sun.
We realize eating's
an art form now, but having
scrambled for strawberries,
snap peas, rhubarb, we're ready
for something we can count on
to stay while our backs are turned,
even if it's only the earthly bones
of something heavenly and flown.

Ownership

With so much shed fur, disappearing bagels,
going out and going out, de-stuffing of animals,

it wasn't a practical move. Some advised,
a single parent has no business. Yet here lies

the advertised pet, unconcerned with the future
despite a past that shows in her posture,

haste to the bowl. Certain favorites had to go —
morning paper, gym — but there's audio

news, and a dog can be personal trainer,
insisting you show up. Mostly, she offers

lessons in stillness, the center that's missing.
And I had begun to believe in nothing

as a form of devotion: the desire to stay home
as if everything outside were a bomb, a storm,

whatever lands a dog in a shelter, pregnant.
Unsure what I wanted, I knew I wanted

this one, trembling, malnourished, eager
for routine. I went through the calendar:

where could I fit her in? I hounded
my dog-owning friends: how did

they know where to walk? None could say.
It happened, they told me, like love, like age:

just leash up, go outside: it will arrive.
To think, last year at this time

I lived in a fur-free zone (though not without mess),
she was in terrible trouble, and we hadn't even met.

Grief

Stray dog that neither
departs nor agrees to be adopted,
it stands in rain and mud beneath

the yew, sometimes willing to eat,
unready to be touched. Where it spends
the intervening days, where it sleeps,

who its associates are, remain unknown,
but it's made the semblance of a home
on the welcome mat. I won't summon

Animal Control, because this is one
animal not to be controlled.
I know from the face. I know from

the way it walks off, it has somewhere
to go. It likes to be lonely, hungry, cold.
It would rather imagine a warmer, softer

life than live one, because then
there'd be nowhere left to travel.
I make sure not to plan for it, even when

going out of town. Neither family
nor property, it seeks to dwell with me,
not in a home, but on a home's periphery.

Sage

Should I plant if what they say is true:
it delivers not only wisdom, but rescue
by eternal life? I'd prize its furry company
after everyone else was gone – family,
fellow readers, sworn companion –
and always be out of date, the only one,
crazy lady ringed by her favorite crop,
ladling beany soups from ancient pots,
recounting how a leaf outsmarted death.
Neighbor kids would flee, keen to accept
the course of things, suspecting thief or devil
in anything that sprang or seemed eternal.
Whoever approached, whoever fled the kitchen
wouldn't matter, nor whether it was written.

The Rosemary, Outside

There's rosemary, that's for remembrance. Pray you love, remember.
— William Shakespeare

Had you any conception
how literary my history,
how classical my origins,
you would never have left me

here on the frosted terrace
in hopes I would overwinter
without help from the furnace.
While none can recover

the dead, some of us can stem
the odor, maintain an illusion
of form, while you attempt
to absorb what has happened:

not insignificant power.
Yet you make me commonest
additive, like salt, black pepper,
always at hand. When first

we met, you thought fortune
had sent me, a gift, awakening,
but now that the season
of generous sunlight is fading,

you retreat to your couch,
oblivious, with novels and tea.
When you finally step back out
it will be spring, your brief,

human remorse a quick stab
as you survey the garden
to which I haven't come back,
and remember your passion.

Tomatoes

They ended this week, close to November,
freak snowfall downing tree limbs
onto gardens, awnings, bikes. Temperatures

had kept tomatoes swelling into fall,
in biblical rain. My scientist friend says this
is apocalypse, we're in it. He's unsentimental –

he deals with it all day, as some do the economy –
but, teacher of English, I'm shocked each time.
I had filed the weather as synecdoche,

along with polar melt, national debt, the flight
of the cranberry north – all fine images.
Labor Day, I blanched the annual landslide,

raced them as they wept on the counter,
bleeding, splitting, growing black spots,
practically moving, punishing procrastinators

by exploding or simply dying. I said in jest
they'd made me farm wife for the weekend,
even cherished the moment of *rats!* I've lost

the recipes I marked in books all winter,
tabbouleh, simple pizzas, Israeli salad.
One day when the world is even warmer,

we'll rail against loss, how nothing tastes as it did,
how "American" could once be said
with apple pie, how we used to bid

our plants goodbye at season's end,
knowing they'd be back – not always where
we wanted them to be – and how we spent

our winters shoveling snow, our summers by the sea.

Mortals

Again we're paying for crimes
we didn't know we committed: being smart
or beautiful, able to throw a discus too far.

Normally we're doing the unglamorous –
answering mail, hanging clothes to dry –
when the thunderbolt splits the workaday sky,

high, capricious wrath transforming us
into rainclouds, rocks, or squirrels to be chased
by our dogs, the orphans we saved

from gas or the needle. That morning
we'd bought phosphate-free detergent,
voted, biked, declined a prescription,

but the gods were incensed. Was it something
cruel we thought, the vagueness of our piety,
distant tragic news we didn't take time to read?

The turning point must have been small,
that leatherbound journal with acid-free paper,
the little black dress, days of clear weather,

a glimmer for which we didn't give thanks,
though we're unsure to whom (it feels like artifice)
and it's never been clear where to leave the sacrifice.

April

I've long had to be the responsible one:
oldest child, wife, mother.
Now I catch myself casting shadows
over all the young plants, even as year after year
they prove themselves to be true.

The season doesn't know what it wants.
It would turn back the clock if it could, and not come out.
It's suspicious of celebration; a jealous god might overhear.

Once we thought we would conquer the world,
but no one wanted to do the planning.
Another year is gone; the children will grow up.
But they are still small, and we not yet old.
What use is the struggle?

Always, the summer comes, with idleness and sweat.
Always, I end up embracing it, despite
its numbered days, its intentions.

The plot fails every time. Why did I work so hard?
I always end up alone
in wanting the end of things: flowers, tomatoes,
perfection, the profusion of hours, as the waiting,
the counting down, become the loss itself.

First Garden

All summer I tried to hold on,
extend the season of freedom,
pictured false springs on windowsills,
a hoard of frozen tomatoes. As if autumn

could be held off, as if I didn't love it,
as if lacking in solitude and idleness,
I dragged out each day, prolonged it
by not enjoying it. This morning was crisp

though mostly summer. Expecting
to mind, I didn't. The sunflowers
with broken necks, stems of bitter
broccoli, tired nasturtiums – everything

I loved could go to ruin. As their motions
and protests have slowly turned legible,
I've been able to pass most days alone
another year, even as the children

move closer to leaving and my devotion
remains in its wrong and right position.
I've forgotten my center, tried to take it
from the soil, always with excellent reasons.

Nothing wrong with loving the earth,
but the earth is one of many necessary
altars. The secret of creation would never be
so obvious. I've got to embrace the fear,

be a failure, act more like a president:
give up the re-digging, excess alertness,
misinterpreting of wilt – killing the plant
that wanted neglect, with kindness.

Inclinations

Minimalist stage sets; mid-list authors;
discarded pets; streets no one's heard of;
clothes in counterintuitive colors;
poems that rhyme; yard-sale furniture;
unpopular children; the end of vacation;
the hour before sunrise; no-name shampoo;
immigrant grocers; TV without stations;
scratch-and-dent appliances; outdated news.

I love the sense of putting down a root
where soil seems not to have gathered.
While the gentleman in the beautiful suit
pretends to be listening, we freely pioneer,
buying Manhattan for a dollar an acre,
then driving quietly west, foraging dinner.

IV

Oh, must we dream our dreams
and have them, too?

– Elizabeth Bishop

Procrastination

It was surely invented by demons.
No one else could make it the human
norm, defied only by those military
civilians no one can identify
except as aberrations everyone
resents, know-it-alls impervious
to temptation, misfit geniuses,
certain as engines. Released into
the world of people, they cling to
order, chronically surprised
no one else met requirements,
complacently holding the ruler
by which the rest of us measure
growth, as we quit, start over,
scale the hills of our failure,
and descend the other side,
telling stories of our lives.

Achievement

Turns out you could be wanted for your presence,
je ne sais quoi could be said without subtext,
and you could visit a country not having studied,
stammering interrogatives, and still be desired.
Nothing against industry here – everyone ought
to do like a Boy Scout – but time being short,
you might just buy a ticket. Stay home if home
is where you want to be, in heat wave or storm,
treasuring shelter, but don't do too much research.
All I did for years was research. My universe
was books. Love and travel found me by exception
but took their time. When they ask me (with affection)
Where have you been, the *all my life* is implied.
And where had I been? I can't even say I tried.

Technology

I feared it would rob me of something, purity,
the ability to listen, solitude, the shape of memory.

I held it off without knowing. Gadgets spread;
I distrusted them all, even in the hands of friends.

Like the old woman peering out between curtains
at the new neighbors with their terrorist moving van,

I longed for print newspapers, knowing what things
looked like, leaving no trail. Someone was watching.

Keyboards evoked my father's typewriter, non-electric,
on which he'd done his doctorate, exiled, homesick.

The aerogrammes on which I wrote exotic strangers
would go the way of those from my grandfathers.

Even languages without alphabets going paperless,
drawing and writing could never be synonymous.

Once they went virtual, where would I lay my hands?
How would I imagine, when thinking made no sound?

How did *text*, which once suggested sanctity,
become a verb, neither spiritual nor literary?

What became of the nation we stayed to protect
when the emigrés set sail, swearing they'd be back?

By the Sea

Wedded to plans, we make them happen,
straight into the eye of a tropical depression,

water halfway up the tires, ferries potentially
canceled. The plan: to find tranquility

between the uphill of going and the plateau
of having gone. That night, the inn, though

waterlogged, serves hamachi and oysters
to an echoing hall. Next day, clearer,

at least one bride goes by: it's that kind of place.
Bowls of perfect apples adorn the hallways;

no one minds directing strangers to the lighthouse.
It's too cold to swim, which puts me at ease –

I'm at a loss in full sunlight – though here,
the beach behaves like a season or color,

incidental, a circumstance. One of us always
remembers the way; one of us has the key;

if only I'd known what was possible then.
Or so we say as rising waters undo more plans,

then make them again, into something else good.
The land wavers. The sky seems to know it would.

On Seldom Going to the Movies

I hate being told how to picture the villages,
dinner tables, the man's body, the woman's.
I hate the attacks, even the sweet revenges.
I hate knowing and not knowing the outcome;
I hate the unnecessary carnage.

I hate the houses, cozy and mainstream,
the shacks full of corruption and dust.
I hate the portrayal of the ideal woman,
the implication for the rest of us.
I have no desire for the ideal man.

I hate the speakers, too close and loud,
hate the absence of chapter or rhyme.
I abhor the popularity. I hate walking out
single file, everyone lately the same,
some affirmed, some in self-doubt,

and I hate never spotting a character
like me, except as backdrop or filler,
nor anyone like you, who should've been there,
taking my hand and saying ordinary words
to make me feel like a movie star.

Land of Plenty

While others called their parents idiots,
tore up clean paper, and hid cigarettes,

I could barely crumple the lunch bag
my mother expected me to toss. Packed

with two journeys across the Pacific,
it looked like anyone else's – sandwich,

apple, chips – but harbored decades
my parents seldom described. If only they'd

promoted guilt, I might have dodged
the reverence that put good teenage

idling out of reach. With other girls
I sauntered through malls. We curled

our hair, pleasing no one in particular.
But behind each afternoon lay the hunger

of those I couldn't see, sapping the fun,
demanding purpose or at least a reason

for staring at ceilings, telling jokes
without punchlines, changing clothes

too often. When aunts and uncles
(everyone Chinese was "aunt" or "uncle")

started pulling up in new cars and time
became our gold, it seemed a crime,

still, to order more than you could eat,
to have so many rooms to cool or heat.

Conscience cast me out; it was obvious
I couldn't feign a moment's carelessness.

What would I buy, not from clearance?
Where would I travel, given license?

Youth

Prospects were too many
once you reached the city.
Lack of obligation
trapped you at parties,
longing to be thirty.

Smart enough to skip grades,
you could have jumped to marriage.
Midlife would have shaken out
the same: independent, slightly
injured, unembarrassed.

Not in need of ups and downs,
you set out to endure them.
Happiness was way too easy,
so you went around the town
loving damaged persons,

being damaged in return,
and looking out each window
for the one who'd lived like you.
You would know when age had dawned.
There would be a signal.

If Only I'd Met You Earlier

We're at it again. It's hard not to rewrite
the years, though we couldn't have known
they were wrong, if they were. Life
isn't longer than it is, so off we go,

picturing what might have happened,
though one of us would have been taken,
or both, and one of us lived up north, one
by the warmest sea. We had no common

travel destinations, we rarely read
the same books, there wasn't one same
friend, and either might have fled
when hope set in. Apologies, if made,

might not have been accepted. In truth
we could only have met on the street,
on one of your trips to the city. We'd both
have held back. The courage to speak

would have yielded "Excuse me," no more,
all vision cordoned off by the sun.
So we might as well indulge in the words
for their sound: You would have been the one.

Radiology

When the tech starts asking questions –
"Where'd you go to school?" "What
do you teach?" – I brace for astonishment
that it's English, not math or Chinese, but

she registers plain delight I'm a writer.
There must be no one in Radiology
to talk to. She seems to hope I can tell her
a story, but all I can muster is the anxiety

that trailed the impact, a week ago, and recall
how I sat with the coldest object I could find,
a bottle of water, on my head – no physical
ache of blood or bone, only the dread my mind

unleashed, its fortresses leveled by the blow.
I knew, without reason, he'd soon be gone,
everything canceled, the future mine, although
we had mapped it together: oceans, mountains,

avenues. Season of flower, season of ice –
wherever I wanted, he was going to take me.
The radiologist hopes I'll talk about my life.
All I can offer is, "I thought bodily injury

wouldn't ruin my work – I make my living
with my mind – but then I hit my head,"
at which she morphs into an angel, admitting,
"We aren't in control of our destiny," the best

small talk I've had all week. All the talk is small
compared to what he will say, the moment
he's able. Half an hour later, the nurses call
me over: the scan has revealed no fragments

of bone. I know they were fragments of grief,
not bone. I must have wept them out that day
when he hurried over with ice in a cloth
and wrapped me in his arms, not quite the way

he would a few days later, when he no longer
loved me – out of ordinary human sentiment,
the way you put your arms around a stranger
you find at the scene of an accident:

commonly, to keep her warm for the interim
until, having moments ago entered your life,
she passes back out of it without a name
and into that of the first paramedic to arrive.

Downward Dog

Through the changes, the forms persist:
swan, eagle, cow's head, warrior.
How many times have I lain in a twist,
attempting to exhale the sorrow

by swan, eagle, cow's head, warrior?
I've failed again to seek what I require.
Every attempt to exhale the sorrow
only illumines the repetitive nature

of this failure to seek what I require.
How many times must I start from scratch?
Someday the repetitions of nature
must end, though the postures last:

how many times can I start from scratch
as bodies pile up? What looked like love
must end, though the postures last.
Again I admit what it really was

as the bodies part. What looked like love,
we were holding up like a bridge.
Now, admitting what it really was,
I also remember the joy, the surge

of strength in holding up the bridge
even as he withdrew the support,
cruel, unburdening. The joy, the surge
of strength are hard to detect as I mourn

but – even as he withdraws the support –
find grace I didn't know I possessed.
Strength is hard to detect as I mourn,
but practice confers it, even at rest,

with grace I didn't know I possessed.
In word and deed, he loved me back,
but practice confirms it, even at rest:
I've lost a thing I never had.

In word and deed, he loved me back.
How many times have I lain in a twist,
grieving for something I never had?
Through the changes, the forms persist.

Learning Cursive

From the Latin *cursus*, past participle
of *currere*, to run, it granted me a single
athletic form, the starting gun
smoothing the page. I favored a pen
that required some force (no gel, no felt)
and narrow ruling, to edge out glut.
Hand and brain traveled in tandem,
enabling feet. Rhymes arrived; kingdoms
rose up to meet the encroaching lines.
Quieter than print but by no means silent,
it cut down thickets of stuck thought,
slashing the under- and over-wrought.
After the race, I read what was left.
Instructed to run, it had once again leapt.

Twenty-Two

You were thinking of the future
all along: that's why you behaved
as you did. You moved like a fugitive
through weeks and months, your age

a talisman against ruin (though even
then you knew better), and nurtured
the favor of those who would never
reciprocate, who'd take your word

and not give it back. And you didn't
even have that much fun: ahead
of the curve, you found the living
obligatory. But one thing you hated

was a know-it-all. And you had to be
ready: what if your life would be long?
You needed more. You needed a story,
a narrow escape, something to reflect on:

stupid jobs, bad company, disasters
professional, familial, romantic.
There was no requirement of failure,
but the alternative was pathetic:

to think out your life in your head
(for what a good brain was in it!),
do everything right the first or second
time, lie down dead, and live it.

Adaptation

Each day begins with the unwise thought
that the drowning could be reversed,
the house un-burned, the thief un-caught.

Distrusting all reason, I got what I sought,
a chance to repeat what I knew wouldn't work,
beginning each day with the unwise thought

that like reading and writing, love can be taught.
I blame it on dreams, in which we're un-cursed,
the house un-burned, the thief un-caught,

and time goes forward and back, as it ought.
We advance without mishap, having rehearsed
our beginnings and silenced the thoughts

we shouldn't have spoken; thus un-fraught,
we live out the fairytale. I know it's perverse –
the house is burned, the thief is caught –

but sleep renders daylight's wars un-fought,
renewing the malady mind would have nursed
away. Thus I begin with the unwise thought
of the house un-burned, the thief un-caught.

To a Student Dying Young
for Nate

My job was to prepare you, to send you into your life
knowing what to read – because no one has time
to read everything – and knowing what to write.

Even if you chose not to use them, you'd have tried
the ancient forms, learned how meaning dwells in rhyme.
My job was to prepare you, to send you into your life,

which gleamed not just with youth but with the light
that surrounds the exceptions, those unresigned
to the brevity of things. Assigning what to write,

I said "Do Not Go Gentle Into That Good Night"
might help: a son who asks his father not to die.
My job was to prepare you for the rest of your life,

so I tended to forget you were already in it, like
us your elders, running down the allotted time,
though reading everything and learning what to write.

Luckily you were the wiser, accepting each day and night
as a gift upon a gift, which is the gift you leave behind.
My job was to prepare you, to send you into your life
knowing what to read. Instead, you teach me what to write.

"To a Student Dying Young"
is dedicated to the memory of
Nathaniel Kirkland
1988-2009

Acknowledgments

Many thanks to the editors of these journals, where the following poems first appeared, some in slightly different form:

Asian American Literary Review: "Bathtime," "Practice," "Sunday Dinner," "Twenty-Two," "When More Is Better"
Blue Lyra Review: "Land of Plenty," "Procrastination"
Cavalier Literary Couture: "Asian Shrimp," "Ownership"
Cerise Press: "April"
The Cincinnati Review: "Raspberry Patch"
ConnotationPress: An Online Artifact: "By the Sea," "Chinese Parsley," "Mortals"
Crab Orchard Review: "1980," "Rosemary"
Dickinson Magazine (online edition): "To a Student Dying Young"
Dickinson Review: "Carlisle, Pennsylvania"
Hawai'i Pacific Review: "Achievement"
The Kenyon Review: "Backyard"
Massachusetts Review: "Grief"
New Ohio Review: "If Only I'd Met You Earlier"
The New Republic: "The Wife"
New England Review: "Contentment," "On Writing"
New Ohio Review: "If Only I'd Met You Earlier"
Northwest Review: "On Seldom Going to the Movies"
Poet Lore: "Technology"
Prairie Schooner: "To a Limited Extent," "Radiology"
Southwest Review: "First Garden"
Terminus: "Sage," "The Frost Place"

"On Writing" appeared in *Best American Poetry 2013*

Quotation sources:

Elizabeth Bishop, "Questions of Travel," *The Complete Poems 1927-1929,* Farrar, Straus and Giroux, 1979.

Stanley Kunitz, "The Mulch," *The Collected Poems,* W.W. Norton & Co., 2000.

Adrienne Rich, "Prospective Immigrants Please Note," *The Fact of a Doorframe,* W.W. Norton & Co., 1984.

Jean Valentine, "Miles from Home," *Home Deep Blue,* Alice James Books, 1988.

For their essential critiques of work in progress, much gratitude to Sharon O'Brien, Jennifer Joseph, Siobhan Phillips, Diana Rico, Claire Seiler, Faith Shearin, and Melanie Sumner. Many thanks, also, to Dickinson College and the Fine Arts Work Center in Provincetown's Returning Residency program, for support in the writing of these poems. And lifelong gratitude to my parents, Jennifer and Kendall Su, who made the first house home, and to the three who make today's house home: Aisling, Dervla, and Star.

About the Author

Adrienne Su is the author of three previous books of poems, *Middle Kingdom* (Alice James Books, 1997), *Sanctuary* (Manic D Press, 2006), and *Having None of It* (Manic D Press, 2009). A native of Atlanta, she received an A.B. from Harvard College in 1989 and an M.F.A. in poetry from the University of Virginia in 1993. Her poetry awards include a Pushcart Prize, a National Endowment for the Arts fellowship, and writing residencies at the Fine Arts Work Center in Provincetown, MA, The Frost Place in Franconia, NH, Yaddo, the MacDowell Colony, and the Virginia Center for Creative Arts. Since 2000, she has taught English and Creative Writing at Dickinson College, where she is Poet-in-Residence.